EXPOSE

the

DARKNESS

Lost and Found

KAYLA MAXIMOVICH OGG

ISBN 979-8-88616-631-6 (paperback)
ISBN 979-8-88616-632-3 (digital)

Christian Faith Publishing
832 Park Avenue
Meadville, PA 16335
www.christianfaithpublishing.com

Printed in the United States of America

Thank you, God, for lighting my path. May this book bring honor to your name.

Thank you, Colton. You not only believed me, but you believed in me.

Thank you to my family and friends who have helped bring this spiritual story into the physical world.

The night is nearly over; the day is almost
here. So let us put aside the deeds of
darkness and put on the armor of light.

—Romans 13:12 NIV

Contents

Prologue

The Mystery

Have you ever looked up at the night sky and wondered what lies beyond the stars? Further than the eye can see, the universe unending. What is *really* out there? The mystery of the unknown has inspired mankind since the beginning of time. Astronauts venture into the vast universe, seeking to uncover new knowledge. Scientists peer into the depths of the sea, yearning to discover what lies below. And miners dig deep into the earth, their eyes scanning for precious gems hidden away in creation. All of them, alike, wander into dangerous places untouched by human feet.

But what happens when we seek to find treasure in depths without end? The treasure is a mirage, always just slightly further out of reach. Obtaining a small gem leads the miner to dig only deeper. Science has not found satisfaction, as new knowledge leads to new wonder. The curious explorer opens the door to the mysterious universe. Reaching for stars beyond our limits, we step away from steady ground. In an endless pursuit to know what is unknown, souls are lost on the winding trails into the vast expanse.

I was once the deep-sea diver, the miner, the astronaut. I reached through my dreams toward the mirage, always just a few more inches away from my grasp. As I followed the treasure, the enemy lured me into the deepest darkest place in the universe: a place where I lost sight of God. For you to see where I am now, you must know from where I have come. Prepare to dive in as this memoir will take you from the inner dimensions of the human mind to the outskirts of the universe. Although I was lost, in God I am found.

PART 1

Lost

It was August 25, 2019. I set a goal. I was determined to make it to the light post by the street in front of my house. Asleep, I felt myself enter a paralytic state where familiar heaviness and the noise of sirens nearly consumed me. Rather than crushing under the weight, I saw an opportunity, a chance to make my escape. *Just sit up.* I forced myself to rise from the horizontal position I was trapped in. I was frustrated to realize that my physical body had risen and not only my spirit. *Ugh. Another failed attempt.* Still, my determination was not shaken. Awake at around 3:00 a.m., I wrote a note on my phone about the control I desired over my spirit.

Writing from 08/25/2019

The things I experience at night are unusual, but I am learning to control them. Instead of surrendering to a terrifying moment of helplessness, I force myself to understand that this is a part of me, and it is something that I will conquer. It always begins with sudden paralysis. When I am sucked down and cannot move, I hear a noise that is unexplainable, a noise I could never recreate. It is loud. It is personal. It takes my whole existence and makes it still, so the only thing I can feel is the pressure crushing my body. Time pauses while I lie there in a motionless existence, waiting for the second of release. I fight for the moment that the blaring sound will silence and the weight on my chest will lift away. I long for the breath of revival after being consumed by my own mind. This journey has been long, but it is not over. I refuse to give up. I choose to learn. I will fight for the right

to control my own consciousness
when it controls me.

My determination grew even larger to control my conscious spirit. I sent the writing to Colton, my boyfriend (now husband), after I reread it twenty times. It's a wonder he didn't think I was out of my mind. And again, I drifted off to sleep.

In a deep slumber, my spirit became conscious again, and I decided to rise. *Whoosh*. For the first time, I felt my spirit divide from my physical being. After rising above my body in a sitting position, I remembered the advice that various YouTubers had suggested for this very moment. "Do not stay still; move. Get out of your room and go explore."

And so I went. Something like a tail on my lower body propelled me through a mystical world in my own home. Although the setting was familiar, everything seemed so lucid, fluid, and elevated. My energy drained quickly as I moved through my house in an unfamiliar spirit body. *Keep moving. Get to the light post.* I attempted to exit through the front window, but I was not able to go through it. I made my way to the garage and melted through the door. Outside, I noticed the sky stretching over the world, its color bluer than any blue I'd ever seen before. Forward, I pushed toward the street. My tail was fighting through the atmosphere to move my spirit further away from my natural body. A feeling of unexplainable joy rushed through me as I realized my success: the light post in front of me, and my body nearly two hundred feet behind me.

I awoke in the morning and looked at my ceiling. I almost jumped out of bed when I remembered all that happened. I instantly wrote down every detail and retraced the path I had traveled in spirit the night before. Feelings of superiority flooded my mind. In my euphoric state, I was king; I was in control. My superpower was being developed and perfected so that I would become unstoppable.

Rewind

Time out. You may wonder how I got to this point. How could anyone in their right mind want to intentionally remove their spirit from their body? Isn't it obvious that leaving your body behind would bring about some trouble? Even if it were somehow pleasant, how could someone possibly pull off such a feat?

To really grip this story, it is important that you know a little bit more about me. My name is Kayla. I was raised to know Jesus Christ in a healthy and supportive home with my mom, dad, and my brother, Michael. I had a wonderful childhood. I thrived in school with excellent grades and had friends of all kinds. In high school, I took college courses and enjoyed serving as the captain of the ladies' track team. We competed at the state meet for several consecutive years. I continued to excel academically as I moved on to college. During my undergraduate studies, I hopped onto multiple graduate-level research projects, helped create an online psychology course, and served as my university's chapter president of Psi Chi, the International Honor Society in Psychology. Later, I graduated college *summa cum laude* with a bachelor of arts in psychology. I am currently (2022) pursuing a master of arts in counseling to become a licensed professional counselor. I am dedicating my career to serving others as the resource I wished I had—well, you'll know what I mean. Yet behind all of my normality, I have always had a sort of secret. Let me tell you how it all began.

My first experience with the realm of spirits occurred at a very young age. One evening, I slowly walked up to my mother. She stood only a few feet from the wall, facing away from it. I hid my face in front of her legs and curiously peeked behind her.

"What are you doing, Kayla?" she asked.

"Who is that?" I whispered, quietly.

"What?" my mom asked, wondering who I was referring to.

"Who is that lady…standing behind you?"

My mom tells me that at that moment, chills crept through her body and every last hair stood on end. With only a few feet separating her back from the wall, her two-year-old daughter told her that there was someone standing directly behind her. I saw many "ghosts" when I was young. My momma always did believe me.

When I was a few years older, nearly six, I was ready to visit an elderly family member in the nursing home. I joyfully leaped out of the car when suddenly, I saw a tremendous skull hovering in the tree at the edge of the parking lot. With empty eyes, it stared at me. I lost my breath at the terrifying sight and nearly collapsed. Once I could speak, I erupted in a fit of screaming. My mom picked me up and held me. She asked me to point to where the skull was. It did not leave or fade; it was as clear as day. I was saddened to realize that no one else could see even a trace.

I can only recall one time in my childhood when I was physically touched by one of the "unseen." Late at night, I stood in the shower. I faced the stream of water. Out of nowhere, I felt two intense tugs on my hair from behind. I was young, so it wouldn't have been too unusual for someone to play a joke on me, right? That was my hope. I turned my neck to look behind me and quickly turned back. I vividly remember the feeling of fear crashing in my stomach. There was no one behind me. No one at all. I burst into uncontrollable tears, and my family rushed to help me.

I cried to my mom, "Why do I only see bad things, Mommy? Why don't I see anything good?"

My mom knelt down and looked into my eyes. "I used to see things too, and so did your grandma," she said. "Something about us seems to be a little bit different because we can pick up on things that other people can't see. But when I was your age, I decided I didn't want to see the ghosts anymore. I didn't want to be scared. So I prayed for God to close the door and disconnect me from that world. That is all you have to do, Kayla. Pray to God. Ask him, 'Jesus, I pray that you close the door that connects me to the ghosts. I don't want to see them anymore.'"

I thought about it for a few days but kept coming back to the same thought: even though the ghosts were scary, I knew that my ability to see them made me special. I felt unique and different from the other kids. After much contemplation, I prayed to God, "Dear Jesus, I don't like to be scared, but I do like to be special. I don't want to close the door like my mommy did."

Eventually, as I neared the end of elementary school, I stopped seeing the shadows. I thought that maybe my spiritual gift had left me or that I was too big and too old to see the ghosts anymore. My daytime spiritual experiences may have come to an end, but little did I know, a world of nighttime terrors had yet to begin. At only fifteen, I experienced my first sleep paralysis attack.

It was January 22, 2014. In deep sleep, I wanted to praise Jesus. I felt my arms rise above my head. They lifted high, reaching toward my ceiling. In a dainty voice, I spoke into the night, "Jesus, I…" then something changed, "*love you*," rolled from my lips in a deep growl that was not of my own voice. Instantly, my arms that were vertically showing praise to Christ were sucked to the surface of the bedsheets. My body was pinned; I could not breathe. A thunderous roar of darkness surrounded my bed as my body sunk deeper and deeper into the mattress. The intensity grew when I realized that I was alone. Darkness had taken my voice. I could not speak. I could not scream. An evil presence filled my room and hovered above me. Powerless to my attacker, I was frozen in agony.

The next day was awful. Thoughts consumed every ounce of my energy and left none for school. I called it "the dream." I tried to tell a few of my friends about the dream, but I could hardly find the words. I searched the web for days and weeks about what had happened to me that night. Most of the sources pointed in scientific directions explaining sleep paralysis as a normal phenomenon. It was comforting to read explanations that were concrete and avoided any mention of spirits. I told myself to believe what I read. It kept my mind off of the fact that whatever had attacked me could someday return.

Several months passed by and I tried to forget about it. Then one night, I was suddenly pinned to the mattress in my sleep again, unable to move or speak. Blaring sirens sent a ringing through my body, and I watched as ants and spiders crawled up my arms and covered the walls of my bedroom. When I finally found my voice, I screamed out loud. My mom and dad came to comfort me. I tried to suppress my memory of this dream, wanting to believe it had never happened.

The voices started when I was about seventeen. One night as I was resting, I felt a pressure on the left side of my bed that made the mattress sink in. A figure crawled up behind my paralyzed body and sharply whispered in my left ear, "*I want you to murder me.*"

I whispered back in confusion, "What?"

"*Just do it,*" the voice tensely growled.

At first, there were several months in between the attacks. But over time, months became only weeks. As events of sleep paralysis grew progressively closer together, I had less time to mentally and spiritually recover. I was scared and confused. I knew that the scientific information I had been clinging to did not fully explain the reality of what I was facing. I prayed for protection, but my prayers did not ease the fear that was gripping my life.

These events became more personally offensive and psychologically disturbing. One night, a man opened my window and crawled into my room. I was on my side when he crept into my bed and lay behind my paralyzed, sleeping body. The man told me that he was going to take me from my family, rape me, and kill me. He drew in closer to whisper in my ear, *"And no one will ever know why you disappeared."*

The attacks were always unanticipated and caused me to panic in my state of silent paralysis. I didn't know what it all meant, but it was clear that I was dealing with a demonic issue. I told very few people about these experiences as they were strange and dark. I continued to pray but found no relief.

Over time, I developed what I call "sleep anxiety," the inability to sleep restfully out of fear of danger during sleep. Sleep anxiety haunted me nightly, and I started to watch my own back. Even in the deepest sleep, I found myself checking my surroundings to ensure safety. This caused heightened internal awareness when my mind should have been at rest. A dangerous relationship developed during this time: with more attacks came more paranoia, with more paranoia came greater awareness during sleep, and with greater awareness during sleep came more attacks. I spent years sleeping in fear, metaphorically with *one eye open*. This cycle was my defense mechanism. I wanted to see what was coming. I wished I could escape.

Awareness Developing

There were side effects of experiencing conscious awareness under the cover of a sleeping body. Aware of my surroundings during sleep, I began to hear music, whispers, and talking in the background. And after a while, strange things began to occur during my dreams that were *not* so scary. Rather, they were fascinating. My dreams became increasingly vivid, and I found myself drifting in strange places. Surely, everyone's dreams are weird. But it is entirely different to be aware and presently conscious during the dream as opposed to only recalling it later.

When I was nineteen, I started to practice "dream-recording," where upon waking, I would write down every last detail of what I could remember about my dream. At first, I caught only snippets of vivid pictures. But as I continued to practice dream-recording, I would rewatch the whole dream in my head and write in depth about the "other places" that I found myself wandering.

Dream-Record 10/08/2018

Suddenly, I was in Mary Ann's car, sitting in the backseat while she was driving. She was headed to Pennsylvania. I looked out the windows and watched the street signs pass by. She did not know I was there, and I kept silent. And then at once, I realized… *This is a dream. I am living a dream. Where am I?* I looked down at my hands to see only nubs at the ends of my arms. *How can I exist here while I also exist in my bed?* (A few days later, I found out that Mary Ann had recently driven to Pennsylvania to visit her family.)

I used to pray every night before falling asleep, but my prayers had become increasingly interrupted by wandering thoughts. Frequently, I would lie down to sleep and "fall into the images" behind my closed eyes. I wrote about the experience of retaining consciousness as my mind drifted away into a hypnagogic state.

Writing from 1/17/2019

"Hypnagogia" Intense imagery floods in behind my closed eyelids. A vast display of colors comes to life and pictures are painted as I walk into them. Hands stretch out toward me, and shape-shifting faces appear. Tunnels present themselves like paths to explore. I choose the green tunnel, and I am pulled in, plummeting into a deep spiral. The shapes that pass by me are bright and bold. Streaks of brilliant color sweep near as I rapidly accelerate. I am soaring through the universe. The speed is intense, and the stars fly past me like snow falling toward the windshield of a moving car. *Where is my mind?*

Amidst my wonderous adventures, I still struggled with sleep paralysis attacks. One afternoon, I was napping when suddenly I became paralyzed. It felt like someone was sitting on top of me, taking away my every breath. A voice of mockery flooded my ears, saying, "Sleeeep paralysis. Ha ha ha! Sleeeeeeep paralysis. *You're helpless.*" I heard footsteps and furniture scooting around. The voice continued laughing at my inability to respond. The heaviness was unbearable. I knew there had to be something more I could do to make sure this wouldn't happen again.

Through internet research, I found out about "lucid dreaming," a state of dreaming that involves conscious awareness and the ability to control oneself or one's surroundings within the dream. The idea of having control during sleep was highly appealing, especially after being powerless to the demonic forces that stole away my sleeping peace. I wanted to learn to avoid the bad times and dig deeper into the good.

I practiced to control my dreams for several months. I learned methods to assess my awareness, like looking down at my hands or checking the time. Doing these things allowed me to recognize my presence inside my dream. As I practiced intentional awareness, I slowly developed the ability to grasp control of myself and my surroundings.

Dream-Record 3/16/2019

In my slumber, I found myself outside with an opportunity to practice control. I said, "I can fly as high as the clouds!" I saw a leaf gently drifting through the air. I grabbed on to the leaf, and like a feather in the breeze, I lifted above the rooftops. I saw the power lines and treetops underneath my feet. Holding tight to the leaf, I soared over the earth. Then I said, "And I can sink as low as the ocean's floor." A heaviness within, I fell into the depths of the ocean and lay on the floor of the sea.

After waking from a controlled dreaming experience, I would grin and feel giddy in my stomach. I fell in love with the control that was growing in me. I felt that my sleep paralysis became manageable as I learned to steer away from negativity. The more I had control, the more it seemed that the demons were fading away. Finally, sleep was beginning to feel peaceful again.

Doesn't everyone dream of traveling beyond the stars? Or wish that they could fly like a bird? I was more than intrigued; I was fascinated with my ability to see what others could not. I loved my mystical experiences in the world of dreams. Sometime in the spring of 2019, I got a tattoo on my arm, "Dreamer" next to a crescent moon. It symbolized two things: my ability to come against the darkness and the discovery of a new passion—breathtaking, indescribable, and entirely unique.

Dream-Record 4/02/2019

I discovered my awareness in my sleep. I was sitting at the edge of a great body of water. It was nighttime, and the water was black. I could not see below the surface. With a fishing pole in hand, I cast my line into the deep waters. Each time I reeled in the line, I pulled strange ideas and memories out of the depths. Yet when I woke up, all my retrieved memories were left at the place by the water. I couldn't bring them with me—access denied.

Suddenly I realized that there was much more to uncover inside my own mind. I continued my research and discovered something called the third eye. The internet explained that the third eye is the spirit eye, or the mind's door to the realm of spirits. It is also known as the pineal gland or the sixth chakra. The sources I came across were full of motivating stories about enlightenment, control, and access to mystical worlds. I became mesmerized with the idea of opening my third eye. I began to practice meditation by breathing deeply and ridding my mind of all distracting thoughts. It was like the inner dimensions of my mind were somehow meshing with the universe.

In continued research, I came across an anonymous post titled, "How can I close my third eye?" I stopped in my tracks, shocked that anyone who was spiritually wise and skilled enough to open their third eye could even think of closing it. Other sources attempted to warn readers of the dangers associated with meddling in the spirit realm, but I steered far away from those. It was uncomfortable to second-guess my actions. I didn't want to feel guilty or scared in pursuit of the mystery, so I convinced myself that I was justified. Although I was spiritually explorative, I was not using physical devices like Ouija boards and tarot cards; all I had was my mind and determination. I was still a Christian…right?

After all the bad nights I'd lived through, I finally found my escape, my freedom from the grip of sleep paralysis. I took control of the thing that once paralyzed me, and I was proud of that. The evil spirits that once lurked around me seemed to be dissolving away as the light of mystery shined brighter. The last thing I wanted was to fall back into a pit of fear, especially now that the universe was calling my name.

Blurred Lines, Deep Waters

In the mind are abstract lines that define one's reality. Psychological theorist Jean Piaget describes the concept of cognitive schemas, which are mental structures we use to organize information about the universe around us. To extend this theory, lines of reality help us distinguish between what is real and what cannot be. When we are confronted with information that seems impossible, we experience cognitive dissonance until the matter is internally resolved. Resolution can occur by redefining our existing lines, allowing new information to fit into the realm of "real" possibilities. A lack of resolution can lead to stress and confusion about the distinctions between real and unreal; possible and impossible. Lines of reality serve to protect the mind so that it can function effectively without questioning the basics.

Dream-Record 6/2/2019

"Waking up in layers." I awoke and rolled over to record my dream as usual. I wrote down every detail. And then, I opened my eyes. I was shocked to be lying flat on my back when I had just been upright, typing on my phone. I checked my dream-record but was shocked to find nothing written at all. Confused, I tried again. I recorded my dream and noted that I had dreamed that I already dream-recorded. And then again, I opened my eyes, lying on my back. *What is this? Some kind of loop?* Rather than trying to record my dream yet again, I decided to get out of bed and head to the bathroom. I needed to splash water on my face. In the bathroom, there were several unfamiliar people. I said, "Who are you? What are you doing in my house?" *Am I still dreaming?* And again, I opened my eyes in my bed. *Is this finally real?* I tried to move my head, but it was like a brick on the pillow. I slapped my face and pinched my cheeks, but my head was a motionless rock. In a trance, I attempted to sit up. *Whoom. Whoom. Whoom. Whoom. Whoom.* In one motion, I rose five times simultaneously. I embodied multiple perspectives that all collided in one sitting position. Seven times more, I opened my eyes before finally meeting my body in the realm of the physical.

My lines of reality were once solid and sure. They were defined by physical laws and concrete possibilities. But as my mind was flooded with firsthand information that did not seem possible, my mental lines became scattered and distorted. Waking up in layers and getting lost in the loop caused me to question what it really meant to be awake. The things that I perceived simply did not fit into the box of "real things" I once knew.

Around this time, the effects of dream-wandering began to appear in my regular daytime experiences. One afternoon, I was contemplating what I should eat for lunch. I was elated to remember the frozen meals I had bought the previous day. I dashed to the kitchen and yanked open the freezer door only to find that they were not there. *Wait…what?* I rummaged through the freezer and then the fridge but still found nothing. My eyes widened, and I took a step back. I mentally retraced my steps and eventually realized that my realistic memory of going to the store did not even happen in the physical world. Although dreams sometimes feel very real, this was a whole new level. Similar occurrences began to occupy my days as the difference between awake and a dream was quickly fading away.

They say you can't die in dreams, but I say you can come close.

Dream-Record 7/22/2019

I sat alone in Colton's car, waiting for him to return to me. I was holding a blank canvas. A yellow school bus pulled up near to the car and several children were dropped off. A young girl with dark hair walked up to the car and leaned into the window. I looked down at my canvas which suddenly housed a painting of beautiful colors; it had been touched by heaven. I looked up again at the young girl and recognized her. (We went to school together, she used to ride my bus, and unfortunately, she had passed away in a car accident a few days prior.) She looked at me and spoke softly, "I know you have thought about me, but you should know that I am resting easy."

Later in my sleep, I floated through all sorts of intense environments. I found awareness while staring at myself in a mirror. I looked into my reflection and noticed dark winged eyeliner on my eyes. The room was all red, almost like a red filter was placed over everything I could see. I floated around the red room, kicking off of the walls and doing pushups off of the ceiling. The setting was eerie and uncomfortable.

I left the room to find Colton, but when I reached him, he could not see my body nor hear my words. I was heartbroken. I sought out other friends and family, but they could not even sense my presence. What a horrible feeling it was to realize that no one could see me. Invisible. Ghost.

Am I...*dead?* In sadness, I drifted from place to place for what felt like many days. Floating through space lost and alone, I finally knew it was time to move on. I turned away from the world and clouds formed under my feet. Warmth surrounded me as I walked through the clouds. I saw the most vibrant blue filling the sky above me. I was saturated by my surroundings when waves of vibration ran all through me. I heard a gentle voice speaking to me, the sound coming from every direction, "Open your eyes to the light." I felt a sense of readiness to accept my own death. "Open your eyes to the light." The vibrations intensified as I prepared to open my eyes to the light. And at once, I opened them, lying flat in bed, and staring at my ceiling.

Many mornings were spent wallowing in existential confusion. Like a dream hangover, the lingering effects were a heavy burden. There is no societal understanding for what I was going through. Imagine calling in to work saying, "Sorry, I can't come in. I thought I was dead last night," or telling your professor, "I can't focus because I am not sure what is real anymore."

Although I found myself teetering on the edge of sanity, getting help didn't feel much like an option. As an undergraduate student studying psychology, you would think I was in the perfect place to reach out for professional help. But how could I come to a scientific therapist with tales of demons and descriptions of other dimensions? I feared that words like "delusion" and "hallucination" would shove my reality into a processable box. I did not want to be diagnosed or medicated as a result of seeing real spirits. I considered seeking help from a pastoral counselor, but I felt that my situation could not be adequately expressed to others. I knew I could tell Colton about my dreams, and my momma believed me, too. But really, who understood? Isolated and alone in my confusion, I felt that writing was the only way to express stories of the spirit in a world made of stone.

I had to do something to clear my head. In my attempt to resolve the confusion, I reworked my lines of reality. I thought about God and wondered where he fit in the midst of it all. God felt distant, and I knew I hadn't been praying as often as I used to. Even so, my spirit felt alive, knowing more than ever. I had never seen God, but I was a witness to my own spiritual ability.

I discovered "New Age" spirituality, which aligned very well with the desire to grow my spiritual potential and to strengthen my connection with the conscious universe. I developed new lines of reality which grew around the ability to control my spirit in the midst of the endless mystery. With some new definition, I was confident to continue pushing forward into the unknown, seeking to obtain greater spiritual enlightenment.

Yikes.

Shattered Glass

I rolled my eyes as my roommates babbled on and on about the Kardashians. The interests of others were too simple for what I had on my mind. As my fascination grew into an obsession, my lifestyle and habits followed suit. My physical appearance and taste in music changed to match my open-mindedness. My clothing was flowy and vibrant, and my brother Michael was convinced that I was a hippie. I got into yoga and started practicing aura-reading. I silently meditated to the universe, casting out all intrusive thoughts. I practiced aligning my chakras, mostly focused on fully opening my third eye. I found that these practices enhanced my spiritual perception, as my intuition became increasingly accurate. The proof was evident in the simple things, like knowing the exact time without looking at a clock or knowing I would see a specific person before I saw them.

Eventually, I developed a dual consciousness where in my sleep, I could simultaneously perceive two perspectives: one in-body and the other out-of-body. One night, I fell into the images behind my closed eyes. I was sitting atop a slide and holding a daisy in my hands. I looked down at the daisy and then at my feet that were stretched out beyond it. As I descended the slide, I recognized my existence in two places at once. One of me was gliding down the slide like a child playing in the sunshine; the other me was lying flat on my back in a dark, silent room.

I continued to research ways to enhance my spiritual practices. I regularly meditated to the silent nothingness, seeking states of altered consciousness. I wanted to induce a spiritual experience. I even slept listening to "binaural beats," tunes and sounds intended to ignite internal awareness. And well, it worked.

Dream-Record 7/31/2019

I drifted away to the tune of lively vibrations. In my slumber, I vividly dreamed of walking on a sidewalk in a crowd of people. The sun beamed down on my skin, and I was warm. I looked down at my arm to see an intricate tattoo of a window, decorated with symbols that represented my spiritual accomplishments. It was like the tattoo was alive; the piece of me that was connected to the universe. I opened my eyes, my body still unawake. In my bedroom were three people, laughing with one another and seemingly communicating with others I could not see. One of them, a woman with blonde curly hair, accurately told me all of the things that had just happened in my dream.

Somehow the presence of people around my sleeping body became all too normal. I followed spiritually explorative writers on the internet who explained that it is typical to see human-like spirits as a result of opening the third eye. I read that these entities were harmless, nothing to worry about. So I believed them—I had to if I wanted to dig deeper. Besides, what's an annoying, harmless spirit compared to the power that was growing in me?

How would you define the word "superpower?" Flying? Teleporting? Traveling time? Many wonder what it would be like to have special abilities. From Superman to Harry Potter to even Santa Claus, society fantasizes about magical powers and individuals who possess them. I believe a superpower is the ability to have control beyond natural human limits—to defy the laws of physics and nature at will. I thought, *The human body is controlled by the rules and laws of the physical realm, but perhaps breaking away from my body could mean freedom to explore the universe with no limits.*

In further internet research, I learned about the spiritual art of astral projection. It is the intentional departure of the spirit from the physical body to explore the astral (spiritual) realms at will. I had heard of it before, but I had always thought it was a myth. If it were real, I knew it would be the *ultimate* test to express my power and control my spirit. Previously, I had only stumbled upon my sleeping awareness or randomly appeared out-of-body. But to step out-of-body by my own command? *Wow. With that kind of control, I could never be attacked again.* From my research, I understood that it was a difficult feat to accomplish. Yet within my heart, it was already settled. In my pursuit of higher power, I was determined to master astral projection.

For weeks, I meditated to open the window in my mind to the other side. Every night, there were people in my room, talking and wandering about. Although they came near to me, I was numb to their presence. Spontaneous out-of-body experiences occurred almost nightly. I drifted to distant lands and wandered the roads to nowhere. I even stumbled upon a gypsy who made a prediction about my near future. In a dream, I was driving along a winding road through a trippy forest when she walked up to my car and said, "In the next few days, you will own many more shoes than you do today." When I woke up, I forgot about what she had said. Over the next several days, my mom bought me two pairs of shoes for my new job, my friend gave me a bag of old clothes and shoes, and I thrifted a pair of UGG boots at Goodwill for five dollars. After I brought the boots home, I put them on the floor next to the others. I was taken aback as I remembered the gypsy from my dream who accurately foretold this strange thing.

A fluid-like connection was developing in my mind, making the physical, mental, and spiritual places seem more and more like one. The barrier between me and the other side was crashing down, and my sight was growing wide. I was proud of my progress but never fully satisfied. Each peek through the veil left me thirsty for more control, more awareness, and more time spent out of my natural body. I was ready to bring down the curtain once and for all.

On August 25, 2019, I shattered the glass. The window I had been looking through was fully open. And intentionally, I stepped to the other side (revisit pages 1–4).

The After

Writing from 8/25/2019

"Choose to feel."

That was all I wrote. My thoughts were consumed, and I was fascinated with the power I held. I was king. I was unstoppable. I possessed boundary-breaking power. I defeated my fears and conquered my demons. And I was *finally* in control. I watched worlds of opportunity unravel and pondered on each and every possibility. I fantasized of experimenting with time hopping, portal traveling, and meeting other spirits like mine in the astral realm. Limits were no longer a barrier in seeking the secrets of the deep.

I even thought to myself, *Why confine my spiritual vision to the boundaries of the night?* I wanted to connect with the realm of the unknown during the day so that all of my experiences may be lived through a vision of higher power.

I was crawling in my skin waiting to be alone with Colton so that I could share with him my incredible success. Colton and I had always joked about finding a portal gun and wondered aloud of alternate dimensions and ways to access them. I was ready to tell him that I held the key and hopefully, show him how to use it.

Finally, the time came to tell him. Colton and I went to walk at Johnson's Woods where we went on our first date. I walked beside him on a path through the winding summertime forest, my mind racing in search of the right opportunity to bring it up. We walked and I giggled; my thoughts speeding and my stomach fluttering with anticipation.

I said, "What would you do if I told you…that last night… I left my body on purpose…?"

He stopped walking and looked at me. "You mean, like, astral projection?"

Excitedly, I said, "Yes! You know about it?"

Colton looked at me with a face of concern. He said, "Don't you think that leaving your body could let other things…in?"

Instantly, I became frustrated and irritated. Defensively, I said, "How could other spirits enter me if the Holy Spirit lives in me?"

Colton paused for a moment and spoke with few words when he warned me of the seriousness of spiritual travel. "I just think you should really be careful. You're messing with something very dangerous."

I was silently fuming. *How could he be so insensitive?* It seemed like no one would ever understand me. Not even my closest companion wanted to share in my success.

A Dissonance

Does the Holy Spirit live in me? I wondered aloud. Underneath a heavy layer of frustration, I knew Colton *could* be right. I recalled that in my internet research of spiritual travel, I always avoided the sources that warned of the risks and dangers of practicing. His words left me without reassurance and rather, gave me a feeling of uncertainty.

My thoughts were loud. *What if the warnings were true? What if I'm in this too deep? Wait! Why am I doubting myself? I have put my whole self into this, and this is mine.* Feelings of success and superiority did not leave me. Rethinking what I had done was not a comfortable option. And besides, I was not finished with my self-praising. I knew the magnitude of what I had accomplished, and I was not going to let anyone take away my control.

Writing from 8/26/2019

This is where I've always been. I only understood bits and pieces of it as it hit me unexpectedly. My connection to the other side, the terrors of sleep paralysis, the whispers, and the intensity of my dreams…all of these things have been very connected. I recognized patterns, developed awareness, and eventually, learned to control my consciousness. Over time, I have learned to live in this mysterious world; a place that others do not know. I've taken this terror, and I've made it my pleasure. For the first time, I have successfully traveled in the spiritual form. With practice, I can see that this could easily be improved and perfected. But is it safe? Not sure…

As you can sense from the writing above, thoughts of uncertainty resurfaced. Colton's words left me thinking about my priorities. I thought about my recent inability to pray to God. I remembered the countless times that my prayers were drowned out by the melting images behind my closed eyes, my attention fully occupied by my pursuit of the unknown. I thought of the many times I chose to dig into the internet for answers, leaving my Holy Bible untouched.

In a dream that night (August 26), I flew high above the clouds. Soaring through the atmosphere, I looked down to see the earth's surface below. I was startled to see myself sitting atop a broomstick, flying like a witch. An awful feeling came over me, and I fell through layers of time and space. I woke up as I collided with my body, very nervous about what I had just seen.

Writing from 8/27/2019

"A dissonance."

That was all I wrote. Intense feelings of internal divide were developing in my mind. A piece of me was worried about how deeply I had become invested in practicing spiritual arts and reaching for evermore control of myself. The other piece of me became angry about the second thoughts I was having. The division in my mind worsened as I pushed thoughts of reconsideration below the surface. I felt the two halves of my mind at war, the voice of reason fighting to be heard.

As I battled between my own opposing thoughts, I came to recognize the severity of my obsession. I thought about the amount of time I committed to my practices. I spent the mornings dream-recording and obsessing over my most recent adventures, my afternoons much the same. In the evenings, I prepared for the night to come. And at night, when I closed my eyes, my dreams came alive. I simply could not think about anything else. My continuous thoughts about spiritual exploration did not allow for patterns of normal, healthy living. I was undeniably obsessed.

Writing from 8/27/2019

"Spiritual warfare in my mind and all around me."

Only two days since my first successful astral travel, I was tormented with opposing thoughts. It was the first week of the fall semester, and I could hardly hear the words of my professor. On scrap paper, I tried to sort through my thoughts but found no clarity. I walked by a poster in the psychology department that read, "Having an existential crisis?" *You have no idea*, I thought. How badly I longed for someone who would understand, someone who could guide me. In my mind, I pictured God looking upon me, waiting for me to turn toward him.

Whispers of the Truth

The cognitive dissonance I was experiencing became unbearable. *What do I believe anymore?* I needed time to think. I spread a blanket over several square feet of grass on a beautiful sunny evening. Tiny yellow flowers peeked around the fringed edges of the woven blanket. I sat in stillness and took deep breaths. I began to relax and let the breeze into my pores. The sunlight beamed through the shade of the trees and warmed my skin. The rich colors of earth's natural beauty touched my soul. I recognized the connectedness of nature as it whispered to me the truth.

Writing from 8/28/2019

> God created everything with its elegant and intricate beauty for us to recognize the complexities that he has designed. Nature points our eyes toward our creator. As I take in the scenes, smells, and feelings of my surroundings, I know that *I am a part of this place and I*

belong here. The brightness of the stars gives only a glimpse of God's light. Rich colors in the sunset are but a whisper of God's endless palette. The diversity of life reflects his imagination. The vastness of the universe is tiny in comparison to God's wisdom. Our God created all souls and all of time and all of space. He has designed every living thing in perfect balance with the rest of the universe. God is real. And this is the truth.

I stood in the shower watching drops of water crash at my feet, tears falling alongside them. Finally, I recognized the reality of my involvement with the spirit world: the spirits I'd been trusting were demons all along. I felt sick. I pictured myself at the bottom of a well, staring up at the faint light that seemed so far away. I was in deep, and I knew it. The door that I had opened would not be an easy one to close. I fell to my knees, "God, save me from this mess."

I waited patiently for the Lord; he turned to me and heard my cry. He lifted me out of the slimy pit, out of the mud and mire; he set my feet on a rock and gave me a firm place to stand. (Psalm 40:1–2 NIV)

PART 2

Found

I was enveloped in a sense of peace, like a wave of light ran through me. The feeling was soft and calm, yet powerful enough to momentarily overcome the division that pierced my heart. I was surely lost, but God never looked away.

The next few days were a blur as I tried to sort through my mess of thoughts. I walked along the edge of campus after class, thinking of the bluer-than-blue sky that existed in my dreams. I looked up at the sky above me and recognized my intentional placement in this physical world. "I am a part of this place, and

I belong here." Later at home, I hung a photo of Jesus on the wall next to my bed.

It did not take long for the division inside to resurface. I thought about my power, the superhuman abilities I worked so hard to achieve. *Does this mean I have to give up all of it? Can't I still record my dreams? How could I kill this fascination?* I attempted to suppress my doubt, but it was impossible to ignore. I looked down at the "Dreamer" tattoo on my arm and felt my heart aching. My ties to the other side were many, and I knew it would be painful and difficult to sever them. I was scared to sleep, scared of the demons, and scared of the open door. I was afraid of my own mind and the forces inside that stood against the voice of reason.

Flick the Switch

Dream-Record 9/2/2019

I felt shivers and drifted off to sleep. A shifty consciousness came over me from the left and right. I levitated but not in a peaceful, delicate manner like I always had before. Something was very different this time. I could see intermittently, and each time my eyes opened, I was in a different place around my bed and in the room. Scattered consciousness.

Several men got into my bed and spoke into my ears. I found myself aware again, but this time I was sitting up underneath the sheets. My body was still lying down behind me. Directly in front of me under the covers was a powerful entity of darkness. My forehead was connected to the forehead of the demon by an electric blue beam of glowing energy, much like a magnetic forcefield. I knew its name: "the Eye." I was infatuated with the spirit, and I felt his heart flowing into mine. We talked for what seemed like hours, sharing our minds with one another. He spoke without words but directly into my mind by the beam, telling me of my great power and limitless spiritual ability. The bond between us was overwhelming and strong; his grasp was overtaking. I turned away for only a second and caught a hint of reality. Realization sent a sharp wave of panic through my being. I frantically shouted prayers when I saw the photo of Jesus on my wall, but by the force of the Eye, I was pulled deeper under the sheets.

And then, I opened my eyes. I heard laughing from every direction. Evil spirits surrounded me, and violent winds blew through the house. The demons whispered to my left and right, telling me that all of the doors in the house were unlocked and that the windows were wide open. They laughed and mocked me. I jumped out of bed, my body still asleep, and hurried downstairs. My consciousness shifted in and out as I moved through the house. I locked the doors and shut the windows that were open wide to the blackness outside.

Awareness returned when I found myself walking down the basement stairs. Distorted mind. I sensed a dual consciousness, as I perceived both a physical view from my bed and an out-of-body perspective from the basement. It was dark. I was weak. My energy drained, and I was helpless. Alone.

Consciousness continued to fade and return in scattered waves. Again, I opened my eyes in my bed. I could not spend one more minute stuck in this endless evil loop. I reached for my phone to call someone for help. I scrolled and scrolled on my phone looking for someone to call, but the screen glitched and was overrun by webpages of evil symbols. I closed out of the endless web tabs, each page showing pagan and satanic pentagrams, inverted crosses, and horned figures, dripping with blood. I knew that I still had not broken the loop. "*God, I need you!*"

I opened my eyes. Shaking and breathless, I sat up in bed. Back in body, I was greeted by the familiar concrete textures of physicality. I reluctantly recorded the painful details of the places from which I'd just come. *Why didn't God deliver me from the grip of the Eye? I asked God to save me, so why am I still being attacked?*

And then, like a light switch flicked on in my brain, I could suddenly see. The entire dream was a metaphor: *I am the house, and it is a disaster.* The open windows and doors were the portals I opened to the enemy. The violent winds rushing through the house were the demons themselves, pouring into the open doors of my mind. Being alone in the basement mirrored my pursuit of the depths, and how it led me away from God, vulnerable and open to attacks. The endless evil webpages represented the countless hours I spent searching the internet for advice on spirit-seeking. And the Eye…it was connected directly to my spirit eye, the third eye located centrally on my forehead. Through the open door in my mind, the Eye was deeply rooted inside, having influence and persuasion over my thoughts. The Eye told me I was powerful, but really, I was powerless to his grasp. It told me of my limitless spiritual abilities, yet it pulled me directly away from Christ.

God's physical creation beautifully exemplifies the power of spiritual truths. In a dark room, shadows hide. We are unable to distinguish a shadow from the rest of the darkness in a room that has no light. But when the light switch is flicked on, the shadows are immediately made known, as they contrast greatly from the light in the room. The demons were hiding in the darkness of my mind, a house without light. But when I asked Jesus to save me, his light in me revealed the truth and exposed the darkness. *God I was blind, but now I can see.*

> The light shines in the darkness, and the darkness has not overcome it. (John 1:5 NIV)

> Again Jesus spoke to them, saying, "I am the light of the world. Whoever follows me will not walk in darkness, but will have the light of life." (John 8:12 ESV)

Research

Your eye is like a lamp that provides light for your body. When your eye is healthy, your whole body is filled with light. But when your eye is unhealthy, your whole body is filled with darkness. And if the light you think you have is actually darkness, how deep that darkness is!

—Matthew 6:22–23 NLT

God, your light has restored my sight. I need you to light the way. I reflected on the many hours I spent prying open the door of mystery and scouring the internet for more. I remembered the man who asked, "How can I close my third eye?" I never thought that I would someday ask the same question. It was time. Time to learn about the truth that once offended me. Time to read the warnings that I avoided for so long.

I hopped onto the internet and researched for hours, comparing my findings directly to scripture. First, I read about the shape-shifting nature of demons, who can impersonate people, loved ones, and even figures of light (2 Corinthians 11:14). I then learned about the *occult*, which relates to magic, supernatural powers, witchcraft, mysticism, and the search for hidden knowledge. A few occult practices include divination, astrology, tarot card reading, reiki healing, fortune telling, the use of crystals to channel energy, and of course, astral projection.

Astral projection is an act of rebellion. Rather than submitting oneself to the authority of God, it is seeking to have control over one's own soul. A person who projects into the realm of spirits defies the natural human boundaries that God has set which were intended to protect us from evil. Stepping out of the physical body is stepping away from the protection of God and directly into the realm of demons. It is rooted in the original act of human disobedience committed by Adam and Eve: those who peer beyond the veil have bitten the forbidden fruit of the tree of knowledge.

> Now the serpent was more *crafty* than any of the wild animals the Lord God had made. He said to the woman, "Did God really say, 'You must not eat from any tree in the garden'?"
>
> The woman said to the serpent, "We may eat fruit from the trees in the garden, but God did say, 'You must not eat fruit from the tree that is in the middle of the

garden, and you must not touch it, or *you will die.*'"

"You will not certainly die," the serpent said to the woman. "For God knows that when you eat from it your *eyes will be opened, and you will be like God, knowing good and evil.*"

When the woman saw that the fruit of the tree was good for food and *pleasing to the eye* and also *desirable for gaining wisdom*, she took some and ate it. She also gave some to her husband, who was with her, and he ate it. Then the *eyes of both of them were opened*, and they realized they were naked; so they sewed fig leaves together and made coverings for themselves. (Genesis 3:1–7 NIV; italics added for emphasis)

The enemy crafts temptations that are set before us like bait. The fruit is desirable and pleasing to *the eye* (Genesis 3:6). But once we take a bite, we are reeled out into the depths, away from solid ground and into the darkness. Without the light of truth, we fall blind to the lies of our attacker. Ironically, as I sought control over my soul, I lost all self-control. "A person without self-control is like a city with broken-down walls" (Proverbs 25:28 NLT). I let my walls down to look beyond them, and when I did, the enemy walked right in.

I paced my room, anger burning in my chest. "Jesus Christ, please forgive me! How could I be deceived this way? *Satan is a liar!*" He lied to Adam and Eve, and he lied to me just the same. My walk into the unknown was accompanied and assisted by the hand of the enemy. In pursuit of new sight and higher understanding, I bit into the forbidden fruit and opened the door to the father of *lies*.

> You belong to your father, the devil, and you want to carry out your father's desires. He was a murderer from the beginning, not holding to the truth, for there is no truth in him. When he lies, he speaks his native language, for he is a liar and the father of lies. (John 8:44 NIV)

My research continued for days as I traded false enlightenment for real light and truth. I came across accounts of ex-travelers who have since turned their lives to Christ. Like me, many of them sought to experience a higher awareness and obtain an enlightened consciousness. Grasping such power similarly turned their eyes from God when they recognized their own spiritual potential. As I continued reading, I discovered the testimony of Steven Bancarz, who exposes the truth about the evils of the New Age spiritual movement. It is not the lovely whatever-your-style spirituality it is portrayed to be; New Ageism encourages divination and emphasizes the lie that we have the potential to "be like God" (Genesis 3:5).

I sat on the edge of my bed and looked up at my dresser. I stood up again and walked toward it, remembering something I placed in the drawer months ago. I opened the top drawer to find a green-jeweled cross necklace from my grandma and granddad. I lifted the cross from its box and clasped it around my neck: a physical symbol of my spiritual protection.

(Reader, I urge you to research these topics,
but only through the lens of truth. Use
caution, as you will discover the writings of
the same godless explorers who led me astray.
There is no good witch or white magic. There
is no such thing as an occult Christian.)

Come Out and Play

Often when we make the conscious decision to better our lives and follow the Holy Spirit, the enemy comes on even harder. He attacks our efforts to hear the word of truth and break free from his grip of lies.

Dream-Record 9/17/2019

Consciousness came over me in my rest, and I found myself hopping on a pogo stick in my bedroom. I was lifted higher with each bounce, floating on gravity of the moon. I lifted my arm and slid my fingers across the bumpy, rigid ceiling. I was stricken with the realization… *I'm out.*

The room became a roar, and I was surrounded by shadowy figures. I shouted, "No! Get away from me!" I fell back into my bed, wavering in and out of body. A thousand shadows stretched toward me. The demons grabbed and pulled at my limbs from every direction. They wanted me to come out and play, to enjoy my superhuman abilities, and loathe again in self-praising pride. The evil spirits were not happy that I chose to listen to the voice of reason.

"I will not let you take me!" With my spirit body, I gripped onto the sheets, exerting every last ounce of strength I had left in me. I felt hands grabbing and tugging all over my body. I started to slip away from my physical counterpart when I became exhausted from fighting them off. I was frozen in time with no escape from my attacker.

Finally, I opened my eyes in the physical realm. I cried to God, wondering why he did not deliver me, yet again. I reached for my phone and called Colton, shaking in fear. I thought of the hands that grabbed me; the figures of black that wanted my soul.

All day long, I was miserable, drowning in self-blame. My mind was drained, and my soul was tired. Familiar feelings of sleep anxiety returned, reminding me of my teenage years when I constantly feared that something was coming for me. I looked down at my tattoo with feelings of anger and regret. I thought to myself, *And I thought things were bad before. Look at me now. The attacks I used to encounter don't even compare. I wish I never pried this door open.* My family sensed my fear and confusion as I told them bits and pieces about the demons I encountered. My dad said, "I wish I could help you, Kay."

I felt inclined to search the internet for answers, but something inside pushed me to reach for my Bible instead. I prayed out loud, "God, I'm scared. I am afraid of the evil that is coming for me. Please, lead me. What do I do?" I opened my Bible and sought verses dealing with fear.

> Even though I walk through the valley of the shadow of death, I fear no evil, for you are with me; your rod and your staff, they comfort me. (Psalm 23:4 NASB)

> In peace I will lie down and sleep, for you alone, Lord, make me dwell in safety. (Psalm 4:8 NIV)

> I will not fear though tens of thousands assail me on every side. (Psalm 3:6 NIV)

> Be strong, do not fear; your God will come, he will come with vengeance; with divine retribution he will come to save you. (Isaiah 35:4 NIV)

In praying and reading God's word, I found strength, comfort, and peace. I began listening to Christian music to keep my mind focused on the truth. The song "Praise You in This Storm" by Casting Crowns reminds me that God is by my side, even in the rumbling thunder and rain. The lyrics explain that my help comes from the Lord, the maker of heaven and earth. I must look to God for guidance and not the internet. "Fearless" by the Newsboys helped me through many nights to come. God is with me in the midnight hour, and I can be fearless in his presence. Phil Wickham's "Cannons" reminds me of my transitional moment in nature; the whole universe is a song of praise declaring the power of our creator.

A few nights later, I recognized my awareness when I was stricken with an episode of sleep paralysis. A high-pitched buzz vibrated the room, and a heavy pressure burdened my chest. My discomfort intensified when I felt the drift begin. Like gravity tugging me from the right side, I detached from my body against my will. As I levitated toward the ceiling, I forced myself to remember that I should fear no evil. Though I could not speak, I focused on the Lord's presence. I prayed in my mind, *God, I know you are here. I am not afraid.* Eventually my sight faded out, and I found myself back in body. Many of the following nights consisted of unintentional awareness and states of heavy paralysis. But rather than being crushed in fear, I trained my mind to remember the truth. Even in the most uncomfortable situations, I prayed, "God, I know you are with me! You have never left me."

In another dream, I found myself in a desolate city, my back against the wall of a brick building. I was hiding from a multitude of surrounding explosions. Bombs were dropping all around, shaking the ground beneath my feet. I found a door on the building and went inside. I ran through hallways to find the bathroom where I planned to take cover. I reached the bathroom and fell to my hands and knees. Bowing to my Savior, I prayed for protection and safety. I stood up and looked up at the mirror hung on the wall. I stared into my own eyes, which caused me to recognize my dreaming self. I looked down at my hands and back into the mirror. *This may be a dream, but I know this is real.* "God, you are here! You are in this place with me." I continued to pray and speak aloud, "In every dimension, in every spiritual place, anywhere I go, God is with me. God holds the entire universe in the palm of his hand!"

Lingering Ties

I intentionally changed my habits and patterns of thinking to keep moving in the right direction. With my cross clasped around my neck, I kept in regular conversation with God, the one who protects me. I began attending church and added to my collection of Christian music. I made lifestyle changes to steer my mind away from its old habits. This included giving up yoga, discontinuing dark meditative practices, and only recording dreams of substantial psychological or spiritual significance. Rather than indulging in obsessive rumination after intense dream experiences, I practiced controlled reflection, where I would allow limited time to process and then force my mind to move on. I removed the astrological tapestries from my walls and tucked away all of the things that reminded me of my addiction. With intentionality and effort, I combated the pieces of myself that were still attached to the other side.

Even still, my dreams remained overwhelming and bizarre. Sometimes, I would spontaneously appear in strange places out-of-body. I came across many portals in my dreams. Water portals, mirror portals, and portals in the walls. I drifted through unfamiliar tunnels. On several occasions, I saw my sleeping body from an external perspective. I often found myself "sleeping on the ceiling," and I even fell through my bedroom floor. The opportunities that I used to labor for presented themselves loosely.

Other times, I would find myself paralyzed and awake in bed. After spiritually waking in an immobile body, I would lay there and think, "Okay, what now? I know I shouldn't move or go about in my house, but what do I do?" I prayed, I talked to God, and I even began singing with the voice of my spirit. All of these things helped pass the time and kept my mind at peace. October and November passed, but still, there I was. Confused. Awake. Aware.

Dream-Record 11/17/2019

Behind my closed eyes, there was darkness. Out of the pitch black, two hands stretched toward me. The index fingers and thumbs of these two hands connected to form a triangle in perfect view.

"Do you know what this means?" a voice asked me.

"No," I replied.

The voice continued in a deep tone, "This is an equilateral triangle. Each of the three sides of this triangle are 60-degree angles. 60-60-60. 666."

Then, from inside of the triangle, an eye opened. I awoke and sat straight up.

This ignited a period of increased awareness of the prevalence of occult symbology in everyday society. The eye within the triangle is a symbol that I recognized in many places. In jewelry, tattoos, and even on the dollar bill, I felt as if it was looking back at me. In pop culture, many artists are photographed with their hands in the formation of a triangle around their eye; it is the very symbol of the Illuminati.

Beyond this, I noticed my friends on social media raving about their astrological signs. In the jewelry section at Target, I saw a crystal necklace that read, "Has the power to cleanse, open, activate and align all chakras." I was furious after watching the Disney movie *Frozen 2*, as it encourages children to go "into the unknown" to find life's answers. (Not to mention Disney's recent [2022] *Turning Red*, in which the main character enters the "astral realm" following a ritual under the blood moon.) Overwhelmed, frustrated, and angry, I clearly saw the grip that the occult has fastened on all of society. "We know that we are children of God, and that the whole world is under the control of the evil one" (1 John 5:19 NIV).

Despite all of my efforts to disconnect myself from the magnetic occult, I still sensed some sort of attachment to it all. I hated it, yet I couldn't stop thinking about it. Perhaps that is the burden of eating from the tree of the knowledge of good and evil. As my dreams remained intriguing and bizarre, I wrestled with a fascination that just wouldn't die. No matter how much I stomped down my curiosity, it remained alive.

Relapse

When an impure spirit comes out of
a person, it goes through arid places
seeking rest and does not find it. Then it
says, "I will return to the house I left."

—Luke 11:24 NIV

It was December of 2019. I closed my eyes and reflected on my spiritual journey. I remembered it all as I once saw it: the intense pleasure of discovering my power and reaching beyond my limits. I opened my eyes and felt saddened to know that it was all over. I was okay with discontinuing my practices because I *wanted* to, but not necessarily because I *had* to. I couldn't help but wonder, *Does this mean my super-power is…gone?*

Only a day later, I found awareness in my sleep. My curiosity was overwhelmingly strong. With little thought, I decided that I must test and prove my abilities one last time. The baited line was cast in my direction. And as I treasured my will over the will of God, my lips were pierced by the hook.

With my spirit body, I raised up onto one elbow, breaking the barrier between two worlds. I rose quickly, just enough to get a glimpse of the room around me. And then, in only a fraction of a second, I laid right back down on my back.

Oh no.

Instantly, I felt a heaviness within. I could still see, and my body was unawake. I looked up. To my right, I saw my Bible hung from the ceiling by a cord, its pages tattered and damaged. I knew what the demons were saying to me: that by choosing to project into the spirit realm again, I severed my relationship with God. But this was not true, for God had not left me.

I stood up and shouted at the demons, "Liars! Leave this place! You do not belong here!" I heard laughing and footsteps in every direction. "Leave!"

My mind blurry, I rushed downstairs to get help. I burst into my roommate's bedroom and found her sleeping. When I spoke her name, her face melted in confusion. She acknowledged me and we talked briefly before she began speaking with other people in her room. I begged for her to listen, but she was fading away.

I fought through layers and layers of reality, trying to collide with my physical self. Finally, my body woke up with me. I sat up and felt immense guilt in my chest. Even after knowing the truth, I gave in to my weakness. No wonder the demons laughed at me! Stepping into the spirit realm and shouting at the demons to leave is like diving into the ocean and yelling at the sharks.

The next morning, I asked my roommate if she remembered her dream. She said, "Uh, yeah actually, you were in my dream. You were here in my room, and I was talking to my friends."

I faced great temptation that morning as I fought the urge to obsess over my ability to enter another person's dream. When I caught myself ruminating excessively, I knew that the enemy still had a stronghold within me.

With my knees pressed into the carpet and my head bowed against the mattress, I asked the Lord to forgive me. "God, I know why I did this. I am still holding onto the controls in my life, trying to direct every move my way. But the control is no good in my own hands. You are in control, God. Only you." I sat alone in my bedroom, remembering the all-consuming division that once tormented my mind. I continued to pray, "I can't have both. Holding hands with two opposing forces will tear me in half. This is war, and I cannot fight the enemy if I'm standing on the wrong side of the battleground."

> You cannot drink the cup of
> the Lord and the cup of demons
> too; you cannot have a part in
> both the Lord's table and the table
> of demons. (1 Corinthians 10:21
> NIV)

Revival

Do not gloat over me, my enemy! Though
I have fallen, I will rise. Though I sit in
darkness, the Lord will be my light.

—Micah 7:8 NIV

Let me guess. You're disappointed in me? I almost
didn't include that last chapter. If I left it out of my
story, you would not know about my obvious mistake.

Relapse.

Addiction.

Sin.

But then I thought…why would I omit something that is so relatable to the human experience? No
one is perfect, and Jesus knows that. Our imperfection
is the very reason that we need Jesus in our lives. The
devil wants us to believe that when we mess up, God
gives up on us. I am here to tell you that is yet another
lie. Even when I fall, God is right there to help me rise
up again.

Often times, we relapse because we believe that we have control over the problem. I thought that I had tamed my sin, that it was under my control. But in sweeping my desires under the rug, I placed a little band-aid on a gushing wound. The time had come to deal with my demons face to face. War was brewing, and I needed to learn how to release the power of God in my life. With the evil army readying for battle, I read about how I could prepare.

> Put on the full armor of God, so that you can take your stand against the devil's schemes. For our struggle is not against flesh and blood, but against the rulers, against the authorities, against the powers of this dark world and against the spiritual forces of evil in the heavenly realms. Therefore put on the full armor of God, so that when the day of evil comes, you may be able to stand your ground, and after you have done everything, to stand. Stand firm then, with the belt of truth buckled around your waist, with the breastplate of righteousness in place, and with your feet fitted with the readiness that comes from the gospel of peace.

In addition to all this, take up the
shield of faith, with which you can
extinguish all the flaming arrows
of the evil one. Take the helmet
of salvation and the sword of the
Spirit, which is the word of God.
(Ephesians 6:11–17 NIV)

This battle is far bigger than you and me. It
spans across all of time and space, pulling on every
human heart. With control in our own hands, we are
weak before our enemy. But when we submit to God,
he carries out our victories. This does not mean we are
passive observers. Rather, "We demolish arguments
and every pretention that sets itself up against the
knowledge of God, and we take captive every thought
and make it obedient to Christ" (2 Corinthians 10:5
NIV).

Writing from 12/18/2019

The strength of the enemy is
too much for me to overcome on
my own. God has given me truth,
and now, I give God the control.
I no longer want to have control over everything. I must learn
self-control in submitting myself
to God who protects me from evil.
In the fight for my life, I come

with the God of the universe, the
one who already holds the victory.
I am with Jesus. He is in control.

Power in the Name

The night is nearly over; the day is almost
here. So let us put aside the deeds of
darkness and put on the armor of light.

—Romans 13:12 NIV

Dream-Record 12/21/2019

In my sleep, I was captured by a heavy paralysis. I carefully thought about my surroundings to keep myself from panicking. In the stillness of the moment, I thought about each piece of protective spiritual armor. I silently prayed, knowing that God was right there with me.

Suddenly, a harsh tugging began on my left ankle. Against my will, my spirit was pulled out of my body by a strong force. I remained in a horizontal position as I levitated toward the center of the room, away from my bed and body. Inaudible whispers lifted up from the floor, surrounding my hovering spirit. Hooked on the fishing line, they were reeling me into the deep.

I heard growling around me as I fought for the ability to speak. In the darkness, I remained focused on the belt of truth and the shield of faith. I pictured God reaching into the depths and pulling my spirit into his loving protection. The growling intensified and the room quaked. I felt the presence of the Holy Spirit, who gave me courage and strength. The sword of the Spirit was raised when I finally spoke aloud the Word of God, "I rebuke you, in the name of Jesus Christ." God's mighty sword struck down and severed the line that bound me to my enemy.

Silence. Stillness. Peace.

Instantly back in body, I opened my eyes. Through the window, I saw the glimmer of the rising sun. The room was calm, birds chirping nearby. I whispered, "The Lord is my serenity." I leaped out of bed and lived that joyous day, finally knowing the weakness of my enemy.

> Therefore God exalted him
> to the highest place and gave him
> the name that is above every name,
> that at the name of Jesus every
> knee should bow, in heaven and
> on earth and under the earth, and
> every tongue acknowledge that
> Jesus Christ is Lord, to the glory
> of God the Father. (Philippians
> 2:9–11 NIV)

I was more than amazed by the miracle I had experienced. Only a few days before Christmas, I was able to directly witness the magnificent power of God. I found strength in knowing that I have the authority to cast out demons in the name of Jesus Christ. But it is not me or my own power that made the enemy flee; it is the power of Christ who lives in me. "However, do not rejoice that the spirits submit to you, but rejoice that your names are written in heaven" (Luke 10:20 NIV). It is no wonder that we are commanded in Exodus 20:7 to never misuse the name of our God. His name is a cutting sword more powerful than even the strongest enemy. And by his might, strongholds are destroyed. "For the weapons of our warfare are not of the flesh but have divine power to destroy strongholds" (2 Corinthians 10:4 NIV).

Writing from 1/07/2020

I have seen the powerful forces of darkness scatter in the presence of the Lord. Why should I fear demons when demons fear God (James 2:19)? If I fear evil spirits, just a tug on my sleeping body or a whisper in my ear will steal away all my hope and leave me paralyzed in fear. The Bible says that we must not fear evil but rather, fear the Lord and shun evil (Proverbs 3:7). Fear of the Lord is not driven by terror. Fearing God is acknowledging that only *he* has authority over all the universe. My God has set the universe in motion. What power could stand against him? I do not fear the enemy; I fear the God who makes the darkness tremble!

The Real Thing

On a cool evening, I sat outside to read the Bible. With the sun setting behind the leather cover, I came across Job 28, "Where Wisdom is Found." I thought for a moment about all of the places that I had searched for wisdom in my life. I sought knowledge in the depths, but my path was aimless. I dove into the universe to gain spiritual sight, but away from solid ground, I fell blind to the truth. So I read on, "Tell me, God. Where does wisdom really live?"

> There is a mine for silver and a place where gold is refined. Iron is taken from the earth, and copper is smelted from ore. Mortals put an end to the darkness; they search out the farthest recesses for ore in the blackest darkness. Far from human dwellings they cut a shaft, in places untouched by human feet; far from other people they dangle and sway. The earth, from which food comes, is

transformed below as by fire; lapis lazuli comes from its rocks, and its dust contains nuggets of gold. No bird of prey knows that hidden path, no falcon's eye has seen it. Proud beasts do not set foot on it, and no lion prowls there. People assault the flinty rock with their hands and lay bare the roots of the mountains. They tunnel through the rock; their eyes see all its treasures. They search the sources of the rivers and bring hidden things to light. But where can wisdom be found? Where does understanding dwell? No mortal comprehends its worth; it cannot be found in the land of the living. The deep says, "It is not in me"; the sea says, "It is not with me." It cannot be bought with the finest gold, nor can its price be weighed out in silver. It cannot be bought with the gold of Ophir, with precious onyx or lapis lazuli. Neither gold nor crystal can compare with it, nor can it be had for jewels of gold. Coral and jasper are not worthy of mention; the price of wisdom is beyond rubies. The topaz of Cush cannot compare with it; it cannot be bought with pure gold. Where then does wisdom come from? Where does understanding dwell? It is hidden from the eyes of every living thing, concealed even from the birds in the sky. Destruction and Death say, "Only a rumor of it has reached our ears." God understands the way to it and he alone knows where it dwells, for he views the ends of the earth and sees everything under the heavens. When he established the force of the wind and measured out the waters, when he made a decree for the rain and a path for the thunderstorm, then he looked at wisdom and appraised it; he confirmed it and tested it. And he said to the human race, "The fear of the Lord—that is wisdom, and to shun evil is understanding." (Job 28 NIV)

There is no doubt that this house has a door. I was created intentionally with a longing to discover spiritual truth; I was only looking for it in the wrong places. Jesus was knocking the whole time, waiting for me to respond. He says, "Here I am! I stand at the door and knock. If anyone hears my voice and opens the door, I will come in and eat with that person, and they with me" (Revelation 3:20 NIV).

I reflected on the days of my childhood, when I feared the "ghosts" that tugged on my hair and the shadows that appeared around me. Even in my fear, I was unwilling to pray for it all to go away. Afraid to lose the thing that made me special and scared that closing the door might compromise my spiritual depth. It was finally time to do the thing that I avoided all my life.

Dear Lord,

Today, I come to you in prayer with readiness to accept what you have for my life. For a long time, I believed that closing the door would mean changing who I am and throwing away what makes me unique. Now I see that you have created me with a spiritual emptiness that only you can fill. I am tired of chasing after false treasures and empty lies. I want the real thing, God. So here it goes:

In the name of Jesus Christ, cut the cords and sever the ties that pull me toward the unknown. Close off the door to all unholy spirits and seal it with the blood of Christ. Let no evil connections remain in my heart. Instead, I open my door to you. May my spiritual desires be fulfilled by your love alone. I will no longer walk in darkness, but I will be led in truth by the Holy Spirit. Transform my heart, renew my soul, and send me to do your will.

Amen.

It was a sunny day in early April. I was twenty-one. I stood next to Colton in church and lifted my voice to the Lord. I was excited to be baptized after service. Done playing with counterfeit magic and ready to see a real miracle. That day, in the name of the Father, the Son, and the Holy Spirit, I committed to a new life. A life free from the chains of fear that kept me tethered to the darkness. A life spent seeking to know the Lord rather than getting lost in the mystery.

†

River to Heaven

The fear of the Lord leads to life, so that one
may sleep satisfied, untouched by evil.

—Proverbs 19:23 NASB

Just as an ex-smoker catches a trace of cigarette smoke, I remember glimpses of the life that I used to live. I still occasionally experience these things: the strange dreams, drifting out of body, and wavering between worlds. As I have gotten more serious about writing this memoir, I have dealt with several attacks. But when I face temptation and threat, I loudly proclaim where Jesus stands in my life. When I remember times of darkness, I am reminded of the light that has overcome it. I know that I am not alone. Because I submit to the all-knowing King, the darkness has no grip on me.

Dream-Record 04/21/2020

I tossed and turned for a while before I finally fell into a deep sleep. The feeling of separation came over me. I hadn't experienced spiritual trouble in weeks, so I did not expect to detach from my body. I fought for a moment, trying not to be pulled away, but then decided to remain calm. I drifted to the right and lightly downward until I wound up on the floor next to my bed. I could see all around me even though the room was very dark.

A spark of curiosity came about, but I remembered the truth and quickly suppressed the temptation. The demons wanted me to search into the unknown; to crawl away from my natural body and remember the power I once felt. But I refused to spend one more second dealing with the devil. I attempted to speak aloud the name of Jesus, but I could not find my voice. I thought, *I am weak, but God is strong.*

I forced my spirit body to travel back toward the bed, fighting something like horizontal gravity. Like swimming through molasses, I pushed through the thick atmosphere. I thrusted my spirit body onto the mattress but could not successfully merge with my physical self. The comforter on my bed was a divider between my body below it and my spirit above. A demonic force suddenly lifted the comforter under me and with it, I rose high above the bed. Quickly approaching the ceiling, I struggled to stomp and kick the comforter downward toward my body. With all of my might, I fought the forces that were lifting me higher.

The demons did this to accomplish one of two things. Perhaps they wanted me to believe that I had separated from my body by my own power...something I used to work very hard to do. And that by the will of my mind, I had the power to levitate, defy gravity, and break through the laws of physics. Second, if they couldn't trick me into obsessing over myself, they at least wanted to terrify me out of trusting God.

I thought, *The power is not mine. It never was.* The voice of my spirit broke through the barrier when I finally spoke aloud, "God! All of the power is your power! God is the greatest!" The comforter immediately sunk down, and I merged into my body.

I opened my physical eyes and instantly spoke to the Lord. "Wow. How many times, God, will you lift me from the dust? How many times can you reach down and save me?" It was like the Holy Spirit spoke directly into my heart when I realized that *it was from the dust that God created me* (Genesis 2:7). I prayed for some time in awe of the Lord. "How blessed I am to have witnessed his power! Who is like God?"

In the middle of the night, I wrote a text to send to Colton. I wanted to share the amazing truth:

Text from 04/21/2020

> The power of God is unmatched. All of the power belongs to him! Every last bit of it. The demons are self-seeking, and they want the same for us. Living to please the self is deny-

ing God's truth. The truth is that by submitting myself to the Lord, no demon dare touch me. Jesus Christ has defeated evil. The darkness becomes nothing in the presence of God. "Because of the Lord's great love we are not consumed, for his compassions never fail." (Lamentations 3:22 NIV)

I continued to pray aloud, asking God to surround me. I requested that he send angels to stand by me so that I could rest in peace and sleep in the presence of his holy and heavenly light. "Your power is unimaginable. Undefeated. Incomparable. Unchangeable. Amen."

Dream-Record 04/21/2020 continued

Again, I fell asleep. And for the second time, I felt my spirit lift from my body. But this time, something was very different. By a mighty force, I was raised high above my bed, and I was instantly filled with joy. I saw my house from above. It looked something like a doll house; I could see into every room at once. I was lifted higher into the sky where I was among the clouds.

"God's love will never fail! God is the most High! Praise the Lord Almighty!" I boldly praised the Lord, my words carrying through the atmosphere. Other voices surrounded me, singing in beautiful harmony.

My sight faded out and I could no longer see, but I heard everything. I heard choirs of angels lifting their voices in praise. Beautiful, indescribable melodies flowed like a river to heaven. I joined the angels in song, and with the voice of my spirit, I lifted praises to my Creator, my Savior, my Lord.

> On my bed I remember you;
> I think of you through the watches
> of the night. Because you are my
> help, I sing in the shadow of your
> wings. I cling to you; your right
> hand upholds me. (Psalm 63:6–8
> NIV)

I Am Found

> Oh, the depth of the riches of the
> wisdom and knowledge of God!
> How unsearchable his judgments,
> and his paths beyond tracing out!

—Romans 11:33 NIV

I look up at the sky, a soft blue; my true blue. Nature reminds me that God's magnificent beauty is found all around me, right where I belong. The voice of reason was with me every step of the way. It was only when I decided to listen that God began to reveal the real treasure: wisdom. It is the greatest treasure in the universe, hidden in the heart of God. I am on a straight path; my vision is clear. I am walking deeper and deeper into his sea of love, finding truth and purpose for my life. Perhaps God knew all along, as he was walking with me through the storm in my own mind, that I would write this book. That I would expose the enemy who tried to kill me and glorify the God who died to save me.

Today, I look down at the tattoo on my arm, and I am reminded of the depths from which the Lord has lifted me. I remember walking along crooked paths, seeking spiritual enlightenment where there was no light. I wondered, *How wide is the universe? What are the limits of humanity?* I yearned to uncover the answers, hidden away in the valleys of creation. But what did I gain from chipping away at the earth's surface, revealing the treasures hidden beneath? I gained nothing, but rather, I lost myself. I admit that I have no answers for the questions that once ignited my curiosity. I now have something much greater: a relationship with the one who knows all things. I am no longer lost in the depths of the universe; I am found in the *Creator* of the universe. There is no freedom found in seeking limitlessness. I have freedom in Christ, whose power is without limits!

Epilogue

Expose the Darkness

Although these pages are winding down to an end, this story is far from over. God has transformed my selfish obsession into a new dream, one worth my full pursuit. I am dedicating my career to shining God's light into some of the darkest places. As a counselor, I will analyze the human experience from an integrated approach—one that acknowledges the legitimacy of science but expands to encompass the realm of spiritual truth. I will continue to highlight the connectedness between physical, mental, and spiritual health, as spiritual darkness is a real cause of mental illness and confusion. Lies stay hidden in the darkness, but the truth is made known in the light. It is time to expose the darkness and shine in the everlasting light of Christ.

Question your obsession.

What is yours? Addictions can take form in many shapes and sizes. Maybe you are like me, and you get lost in the unknowns of life. Perhaps you trade spiritual eternity for material gain. Or you hide from the truth behind substance abuse. Some serve the dollar bill, and many serve themselves. Whatever your obsession is, it serves the same purpose: distraction and deception. The devil serves you the "apple of your *eye*" to keep your eyes off of God. But do not be fooled, for "No one can serve two masters. Either you will hate the one and love the other, or you will be devoted to the one and despise the other..." (Matthew 6:24 NIV).

Believe.

Despite what society tells you, the realm of spirits is very real. Evil hides in plain sight by introducing itself, exaggerating its appearance, and then diminishing its existence to that of a myth. Our society teaches us that a witch is an old grimy woman with green skin and a warped, warty nose. We picture her wearing a black cape, a pointy hat, and flying on a broomstick. Yet after learning this, we are led to believe that witches are of a mythical nature and that none exist in the modern era. Think of society's innocent little depiction of the devil, a harmless red guy with itty bitty horns and a pointy tail. The enemy has a way of presenting himself and then reducing his potency so that he is digestible, dismissible, and unrecognizable. The devil's darkest lie is that he does not exist.

You are not alone.

I am not the only person who has struggled with spirit-seeking and astral projection, for "No temptation has overtaken you except what is common to mankind" (1 Corinthians 10:13 NIV). Whether or not you have dabbled in the occult, it is very likely that you know someone who has. According to a Newsweek article written by Benjamin Fearnow (2018), more than 1.5 million people are admittedly involved in occult practices in America alone. Given the hidden nature of the occult (secret practices), research on this topic is sparse and certainly underestimates the accurate numbers. I am not a part of this statistic. How many more, then, are there? How many teens are clinging to crystals, swearing by their healing powers, or scrolling on live social media to discover demonic reiki "healing" and tarot readings? How many individuals are placing their trust in evil "spirit guides?" And how many souls are in desperate need of help, feeling that no one will ever believe or understand?

The scripture in 1 Corinthians continues, "And God is faithful; he will not let you be tempted beyond what you can bear. But when you are tempted, he will also provide a way out so that you can endure

it. Therefore, my dear friends, flee from idolatry"
(1 Corinthians 10:13–14 NIV).

Wake up.

We live in a society that ignores the existence
of the human spirit and subsequently dismisses the
importance of living in spiritual truth. To no surprise,
this is exactly how the devil wants it to be. The occult
thrives in secret places, where there is no light. This
secrecy can stand no longer with the awareness that
is coming. It's time to flick the switch and expose the
darkness with the everlasting light of Jesus Christ. Just
as we turn on a light to expose what is unseen in a
dark room, the light of Christ can enter us and do the
same. What about your house? Invite Jesus to shine
his light in your heart and open your eyes to the truth.

> Have nothing to do with the
> fruitless deeds of darkness, but
> rather expose them. (Ephesians
> 5:11 NIV)

God's will > my will.

Satan was thrown down from heaven when he
became impressed with his own power, choosing to
serve himself rather than the Lord who created him.
The enemy does not have to get us to worship obvious demons, he only has to lead us to worship our-

selves. For so long, I fought for the ability to control my soul. Turns out, God has already gifted you and me with this capability. Your free will is your power to determine where you stand in the war of all eternity. Place your life in the hands of the Savior. The King of Creation. The Keeper of Wisdom. The Master of the Universe.

Glossary

Astral projection (n.) 1. An intentional out-of-body experience in which the conscious "spirit body" separates from the physical body and is capable of traveling throughout the universe.

Chakras (pl. n.) The seven centers of spiritual energy believed (by some religions) to exist within the human body.

Dissonance (n.) A psychological conflict resulting from incongruous beliefs and attitudes held simultaneously.

Divination (n.) The art of knowing hidden things by means of communication with occult forces.

Hypnagogia (n.) A state of consciousness that occurs at sleep onset, accompanied by auditory, tactile, and/ or visual hallucinations.

Idolatry (n.) 1. Excessive or blind adoration, reverence, devotion, etc. 2. The worship of objects, nature, or the self in place of the one true God.

Lucid Dreaming (n.) 1. A conscious state of dreaming. 2. The ability to control of oneself or one's surroundings to some degree within a dream.

New Age Spirituality (n.) A broad group of spiritual beliefs that promote discovering higher awareness and growing the spiritual potential of the self.

Occult (n.) 1. Relating to supernatural or magical influences, agencies, or occurrences. (adj.) 2. Secret; disclosed; hidden.

Out-of-body experience (n.) A dissociative separation from the physical body.

Rumination (n.) A cycle of repetitive or obsessive thoughts about a situation or idea that can lead to maladaptive cognitive functioning.

Third eye (n.) 1. Perceived source of intuition and spiritual insight, located centrally above the brows 2. The mind's eye. 3. The sixth chakra.

Note: Definitions were retrieved in part from various sources. Some have been adapted and modified to fit the context of this book.

References

https://www.merriam-webster.com/
https://www.thefreedictionary.com/
https://reasonsforjesus.com/
https://www.newsweek.com/witchcraft-wiccans-mysticism-astrology-witches-millennials-pagans-religion-1221019

Songs
"Cannons"—Phil Wickham
"Praise You in This Storm"—Casting Crowns
"Fearless"—Newsboys

Scriptures were chosen from multiple versions of the Holy Bible including:

- NIV
- NLT
- NASB
- ESV

About the Author

Kayla Maximovich Ogg, twenty-three, is a Christian, wife, and student with a serious desire to share the truth. In 2020, she graduated *summa cum laude* with a bachelor of arts in psychology. During her undergraduate studies, Kayla participated in graduate-level research, assisted in the creation of an online psychology course, and later served as the chapter president of Psi Chi, the International Honor Society in Psychology, at her university. Kayla is currently (2022) pursuing a master of arts in clinical mental health counseling to become a licensed professional counselor. In her career, Kayla aims to serve others as the resource she once needed by shining light on the connectedness of spiritual and mental health. In her free time, she writes to bring awareness of spiritual truths into the physical world.

You can support Kayla's mission to Expose the Darkness by contributing any amount: